New Girl in School

Christine Lindop

Name ____________________

Age ____________________

Class ____________________

سرشناسه: لینداپ، کریسیتن
Lindop, Christine

عنوان و پدیدآور: New Girl in School: Activity Book/ Christine Lindop.

مشخصات نشر: تهران: کتابدوستان، ۱۳۸۷.، = ۲۰۰۸م.

مشخصات ظاهری: ۱٤، ۲٥ ص.: مصور.

وضعیت فهرست‌نویسی: فیپا.

یادداشت: انگلیسی.

یادداشت: افست از روی چاپ ۲۰۰۵: دانشگاه آکسفورد.

یادداشت: گروه سنی: الف، ب [صحیح: ب].

آوانویسی عنوان: نیوگرل این اسکول...

موضوع: زبان انگلیسی -- راهنمای آموزشی (ابتدایی).

رده‌بندی کنگره: PE ۱۰٦٥/ل۹ن۹ ۱۳۸۷

رده‌بندی دیویی: ٤۲۸/۲

شماره کتابشناسی ملی: ۱۲۳۹۹٦۱

New Girl in School، نویسنده: Christine Lindop، لیتوگرافی: رهنما، چاپ: چاپخانه نقره‌فام، چاپ دوم: ۱۳۹۱، تیراژ: ۵۰۰۰ نسخه، ناشر: انتشارات کتابدوستان، مرکز پخش: انتشارات رهنما، آدرس: مقابل دانشگاه تهران، خیابان فروردین، نبش خیابان شهدای ژاندارمری، پلاک ۱۱۲، تلفن: ۶۶۴۰۰۹۲۷ ، ۶۶۴۱۶۶۰۴ ، ۶۶۴۸۱۶۶۲ ، فاکس: ۶۶۴۶۷۴۲۴ ، فروشگاه رهنما، سعادت‌آباد، خیابان علامه طباطبایی جنوبی، بین ۴۰ و ۴۲ شرقی پلاک ۲۹، تلفن: ۸۸۶۹۴۱۰۲ ، آدرس فروشگاه شماره ۴: خیابان پیروزی نبش خیابان سوم نیروی هوایی، تلفن: ۷۷۴۸۲۵۰۵، نمایشگاه کتاب رهنما، مقابل دانشگاه تهران پاساژ فروزنده، تلفن: ۶۶۹۵۰۹۵۷

قیمت: ۲۵۰۰۰ ریال

Reading Dolphins
Notes for teachers & parents

Using the book

1 Begin by looking at the first story page (page 2). Look at the picture and ask questions about it. Then read the story text under the picture with your students. Use section 1 of the CD for this if possible.

2 Teach and check the understanding of any new vocabulary. Note that some of the words are in the **Picture Dictionary** at the back of the book.

3 Now look at the activities on the right-hand page. Show the example to the students and instruct them to complete the activities. This may be done individually, in pairs, or as a class.

4 Do the same for the remaining pages of the book.

5 Retell the whole story more quickly, reinforcing the new vocabulary. Section 2 of the CD can help with this.

6 If possible, listen to the expanded story (section 3 of the CD). The students should follow in their books.

7 When the book is finished, use the **Picture Dictionary** to check that students understand and remember new vocabulary. Section 4 of the CD can help with this.

Using the CD

The CD contains four sections.

1 The story told slowly, with pauses. Use this during the first reading. It may also be used for "Listen and repeat" activities at any point.

2 The story told at normal speed. This should be used once the students have read the book for the first time.

3 The expanded story. The story is told in a longer version. This will help the students understand English when it is spoken faster, as they will now know the story and the vocabulary.

4 Vocabulary. Each word in the **Picture Dictionary** is spoken and then used in a simple sentence.

“Emma, this is Linda,” said Miss Taylor. “She’s a new student. Please take her to Class 4C.”

“Yes, Miss Taylor. I like your bag, Linda.”

“Thank you.”

Complete the sentences.

Use these words:

bag	Class	Linda	in
is	moon	black	new

1. This ___is___ Linda.
2. She is a ________ student.
3. Emma is in ________ 4C.
4. She likes Linda's ________.
5. Miss Taylor is ________ the office.
6. Emma takes ________ to Class 4C.
7. Linda's bag is ________.
8. There is a ________ on Linda's bag.

"What are you painting, Linda?" asked Peter.

"I'm painting some flowers."

"Wow! How do you do that?"

"I look at the brushes, then I look at the paint."

Connect.

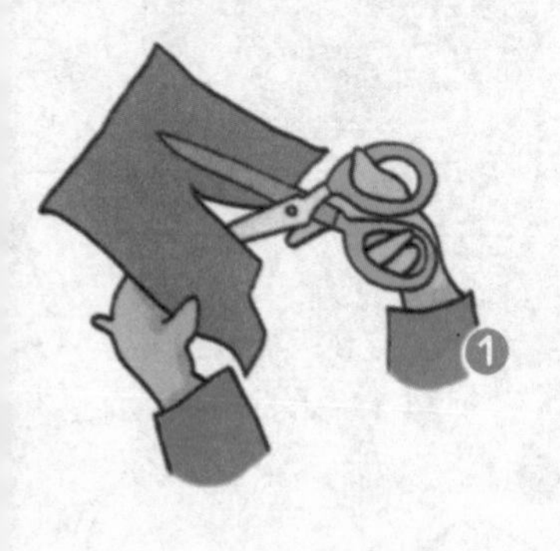

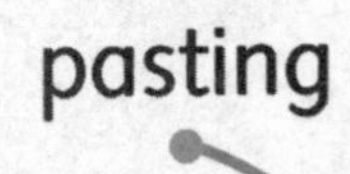

pasting

cutting

drawing

making

folding

painting

writing

coloring

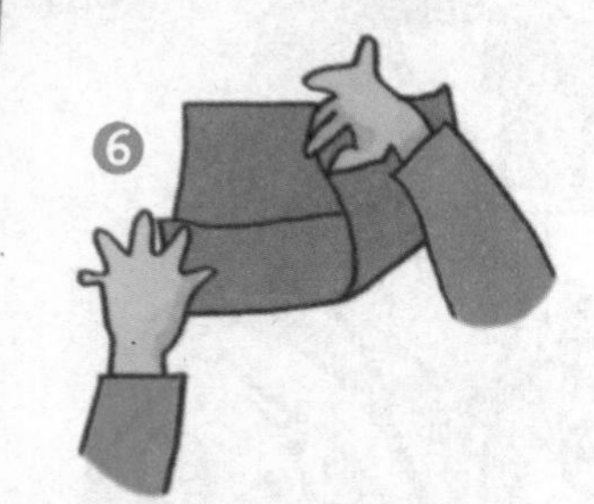

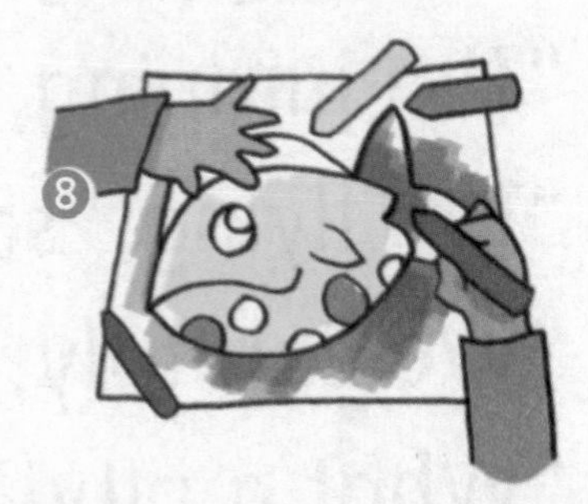

The children were in the yard.
"I'm skipping," said Emma.
"I'm jumping," said Peter.
"I'm flying," said Linda. "Fly with me."
"We can't fly, Linda!"
"What a pity!"

Answer the questions.

1. Are they in the classroom?

   No, they __aren't__.

2. Is Peter jumping?

   Yes, he __________.

3. Can Linda fly?

   Yes, she __________.

4. Are they in the yard?

   __________, they __________.

5. Is Linda skipping?

   No, __________ __________.

6. Can Peter fly?

   __________, __________ __________.

"Let's play some music," said Linda.
"I can play the piano, the violin,
and the drums."
"I can play the flute," said Emma.
"I can play the guitar," said Peter.
"Let's go," said Linda.

What are they doing? Write.

"I'm very hungry," said Linda.

"I want a cookie. Emma and Peter, do you want a cookie, too?"

"Yes please, Linda," they said.

"Here you are. One for you, one for you, and one for me."

Complete the sentences.

❶ I'm hungry.

I want a banana.

❷ I'm ______.

I want a ______.

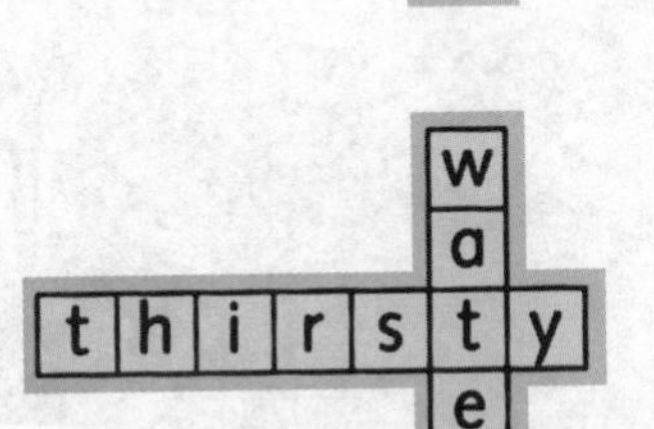

❸ I'm ______.

I want some

______.

b o o t s / s n o w y

❹ It's ______.

I want some

______.

❺ I'm ______.

I want to

______.

"Linda, why are there ducks on your desk?" asked Mrs. Young.

"I'm counting, Mrs. Young. Two frogs and three frogs is five frogs. How many ducks are there? One, two, three, four..."

Complete the sentences.

1. Two plus four is six.
2. Four plus three is __________.
3. Nine minus seven is __________.
4. Seven minus one is __________.
5. Six plus seven is __________.
6. Fifteen minus four is __________.
7. Eight plus six is __________.
8. Twelve minus two is __________.
9. Ten minus one is __________.
10. Five plus three is __________.

"Can you play basketball, Linda?" asked Peter.

"Yes, I can, Peter. Watch."

"Ouch! That's my knee."

"Ouch! That's my elbow."

"Ouch! That's my head."

Complete the words. Connect.

h e a d

e _ _

n _ s _

m _ _ t _

s _ o u _ _ _ _ _

e _ _ _ _

h _ _ _

l _ _

k n _ _

f _ _ _

"What a mess! Let's help the teacher," said Emma.

"OK. You put the chairs back, and I can put the books away."

"Thank you, girls," said Mrs. Young. "That's great!"

Complete.

1. She is ___cleaning___ the board.
2. She is ______________ the paints.
3. He is ______________ the markers.
4. He is ______________ the floor.
5. She is ______________ the window.
6. He is ______________ the books.
7. She is ______________ the lights.
8. He is ______________ the chairs.

"Linda, please come to the office," said Miss Taylor. "Now, where did she go?"

"I'm here, Miss Taylor. I'm in the office!"

Complete.

1. She is reading in the library.

2. She is working in the ________.

3. They are playing in the ________.

4. He is ________ in the bathroom.

5. He is ________ in the swimming pool.

6. She is studying in the ________.

“Hello, Mom,” said Linda. “What’s the matter?”

“I’m sorry, Linda,” said her Mom. “This is the wrong school for you. You must go to the Magic School, not this school.”

Complete the form for your class.

School: ____________________

Name: ____________________

Class number: ____________________

Number of students: ____________________

Number of boys: ____________________

Number of girls: ____________________

Teacher's name: ____________________

Grade: ____________________

"I'm going to my new school now," said Linda. "Goodbye, Emma and Peter. Goodbye, Class 4C. Goodbye Mrs. Young."

"Goodbye, Linda. It was fun!"

Put the sentences in order. Number them 1 to 8.

- [ ] They ate cookies.
- [ ] Emma took Linda to Class 4C.
- [ ] Linda went to the Magic School.
- [1] Linda came to school.
- [ ] They played basketball.
- [ ] They played some music.
- [ ] They did some painting.
- [ ] They put back chairs and put away books.

Picture Dictionary

brush
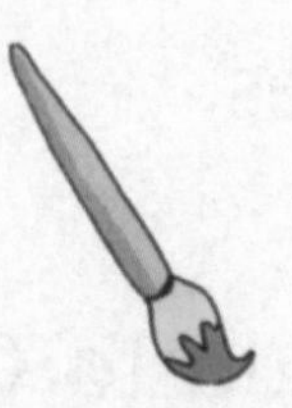

fold

classroom

guitar

cut

head

drums

knee

flute
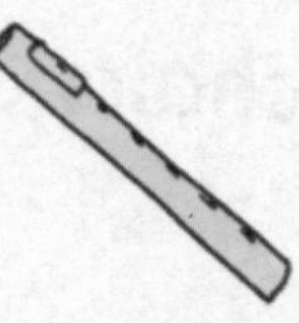

marker

paste

swim

piano

switch off

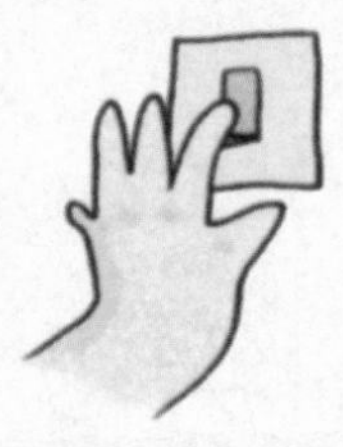

shoulder

trumpet

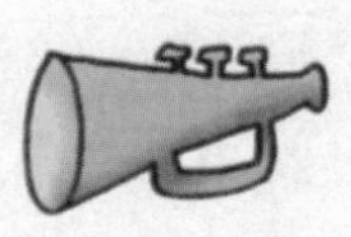

skip

violin

sweep

Dolphin Readers are available at five levels, from Starter to 4.

The Dolphins series covers four major themes:

Grammar, Living Together, The World Around Us, Science and Nature.

For each theme, there are two titles at every level.

Activity Books are available for all Dolphins.

All Dolphins are available on audio CD.
(2 TITLES ON EACH CD SEE TABLE BELOW)

Teacher's Notes are available at **www.oup.com/elt/dolphins**

	Grammar	Living Together	The World Around Us	Science and Nature
Starter	• Silly Squirrel • Monkeying Around	• My Family • A Day with Baby	• Doctor, Doctor • Moving House	• A Game of Shapes • Baby Animals
Level 1	• Meet Molly • Where Is It?	• Little Helpers • Jack the Hero	• On Safari • Lost Kitten	• Number Magic • How's the Weather?
Level 2	• Double Trouble • Super Sam	• Candy for Breakfast • Lost!	• A Visit to the City • Matt's Mistake	• Numbers, Numbers Everywhere • Circles and Squares
Level 3	• Students in Space • What Did You Do Yesterday?	• New Girl in School • Uncle Jerry's Great Idea	• Just Like Mine • Wonderful Wild Animals	• Things That Fly • Let's Go to the Rainforest
Level 4	• The Tough Task • Yesterday, Today and Tomorrow	• We Won the Cup • Up and Down	• Where People Live • City Girl, Country Boy	• In the Ocean • Go, Gorillas, Go

New Girl in School

Activity Book

Name ______________________

Age ______________________

Class ______________________

Before reading

Connect.

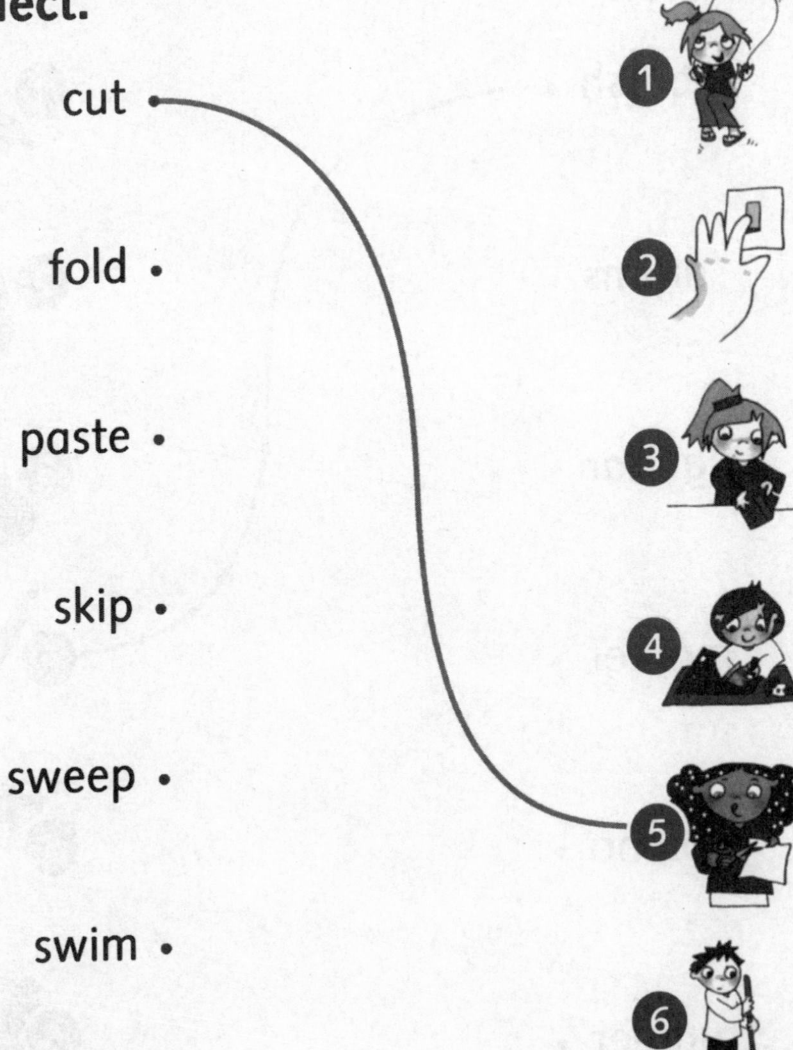

Before reading

Connect.

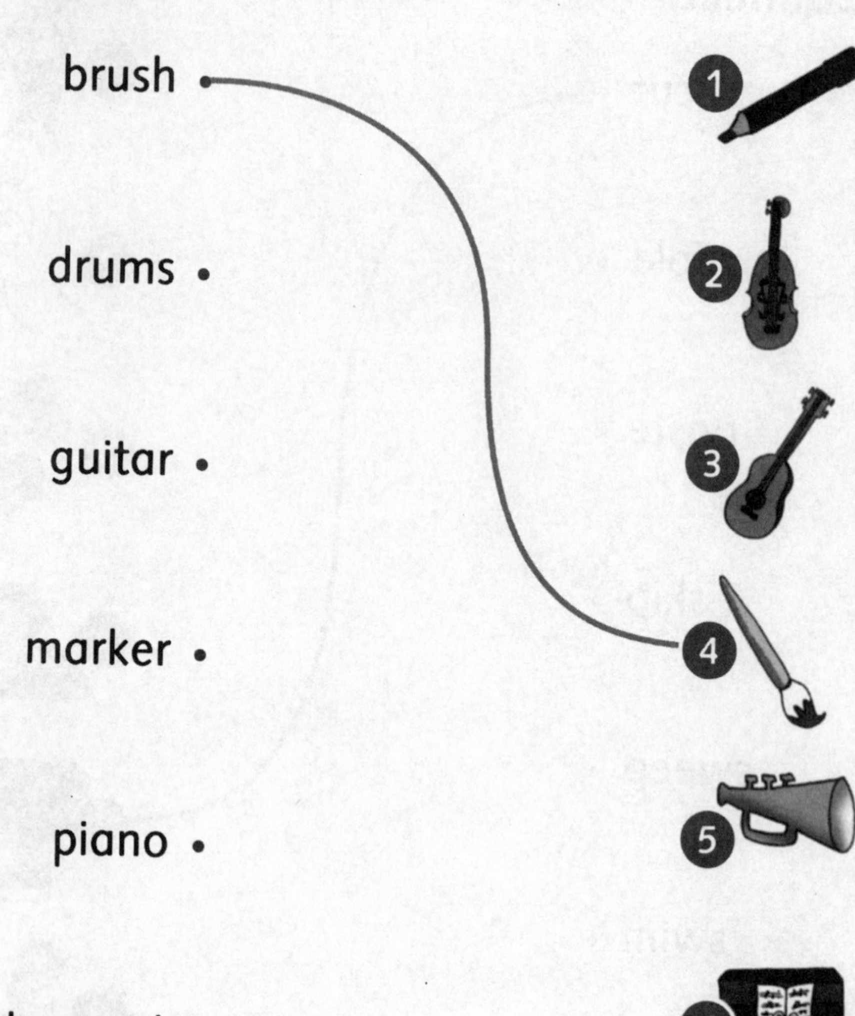

brush

drums

guitar

marker

piano

trumpet

violin

1 Circle the odd one out.

❶	orange	student	banana	apple
❷	shoe	hat	jeans	office
❸	dog	cat	moon	frog
❹	take	desk	sofa	chair
❺	blue	yellow	black	like
❻	noses	looks	eyes	ears

2 Complete using the circled words.

Linda is a new ___student___. She is in the ______ with Miss Taylor. There is a ______ on Linda's bag. "Please ______ Linda to Class 4C," says Miss Taylor. "I ______ your bag, Linda," says Emma. The cat ______ at Linda.

Circle the correct words.

1. Linda, Peter, and Emma are painting / cutting / folding.
2. Emma is painting a dog / cat / horse.
3. There are clouds / moons / stars in Linda's hair.
4. The cat is near the table / brush / window.
5. There are six pictures of trees / trains / trucks.
6. Emma's eyes are blue / green / brown.
7. Emma looks at the birds / brushes / board.
8. Then she looks at the paint / pen / paper.
9. There are three / five / seven brushes.

Circle yes or no.

1. The children are in the yard. yes no
2. Peter is skipping. yes no
3. Linda is flying. yes no
4. Peter and Emma can't fly. yes no
5. The children are looking at Emma. yes no
6. The cat is looking at the birds. yes no
7. One girl is pointing at Linda. yes no
8. There are six birds in the tree. yes no
9. There are four boys in the yard. yes no

1 Complete the puzzle.

What is the secret word? ____________________

2 Answer the questions.

Can you play the piano? ____________________

Can you play the guitar? ____________________

Can you play the drums? ____________________

Circle yes or no.

1. The cat is eating pizza. yes no
2. The children are in the lunchroom. yes no
3. There is a cookie near Emma's head. yes no
4. Peter is sitting next to Linda. yes no
5. There is a clock on the table. yes no
6. The children are looking at the cookies. yes no
7. Linda is very hungry. yes no
8. There is a drink in Peter's hand. yes no
9. Linda makes six cookies. yes no

Answer the questions.

1. How many frogs are there? five
2. How many ducks are there? ____________
3. How many brown birds are there?
   ____
4. How many cats are there? ____________
5. How many teachers are there?
   ____
6. How many brushes are there? ____________
7. How many children are there? ____________
8. How many bags are there? ____________
9. How many butterflies are there?
   ____
10. How many red stars are there?
    ____

Connect.

❶ The children are •	• the books.
❷ They are helping •	• thank you.
❸ Emma puts •	• in the library.
❹ Linda puts •	• under Peter's arm.
❺ Mrs. Young says •	• the chairs back.
❻ The cat is •	• near the door.
❼ There is a green book •	• on a chair.
❽ There are five books •	• in Linda's arms.
❾ Peter is collecting •	• the teacher.
❿ Two girls are •	• the books away.

Complete the sentences.

in   wrong   mom   ~~Class 4C~~   must
desk   skirt   brushes   office   stars

1. Miss Taylor goes to Class 4C.
2. Linda is not at her ______.
3. Linda is in the ______.
4. Linda's bag is ______ her hand.
5. The ______ are in Linda's bag.
6. Linda's ______ is in the office too.
7. She has a beautiful purple ______.
8. There are ______ in her eyes.
9. Linda is at the ______ school.
10. She ______ go to the Magic School.

Pages 22–23

Circle yes **or** no **.**

❶ Linda and her mother are flying. yes no

❷ They are saying hello. yes no

❸ They are going to the Magic School. yes no

❹ The cat is sleeping. yes no

❺ The children are playing basketball. yes no

❻ The children are saying goodbye. yes no

❼ Mrs. Young is in the office. yes no

❽ Miss Taylor is in the yard. yes no

❾ The children had a good time. yes no

After reading

Answer the questions.

1. Where does Emma take Linda?
   She takes her to Class 4C.
   ____
2. How does Linda paint flowers?
   ____
3. What does Linda do in the yard?
   ____
4. What does Peter play?
   ____
5. What can you see on Linda's desk?
   ____
6. Who puts the books away?
   ____
7. Where must Linda go?
   ____
8. How does she go there?
   ____

Complete the crossword.

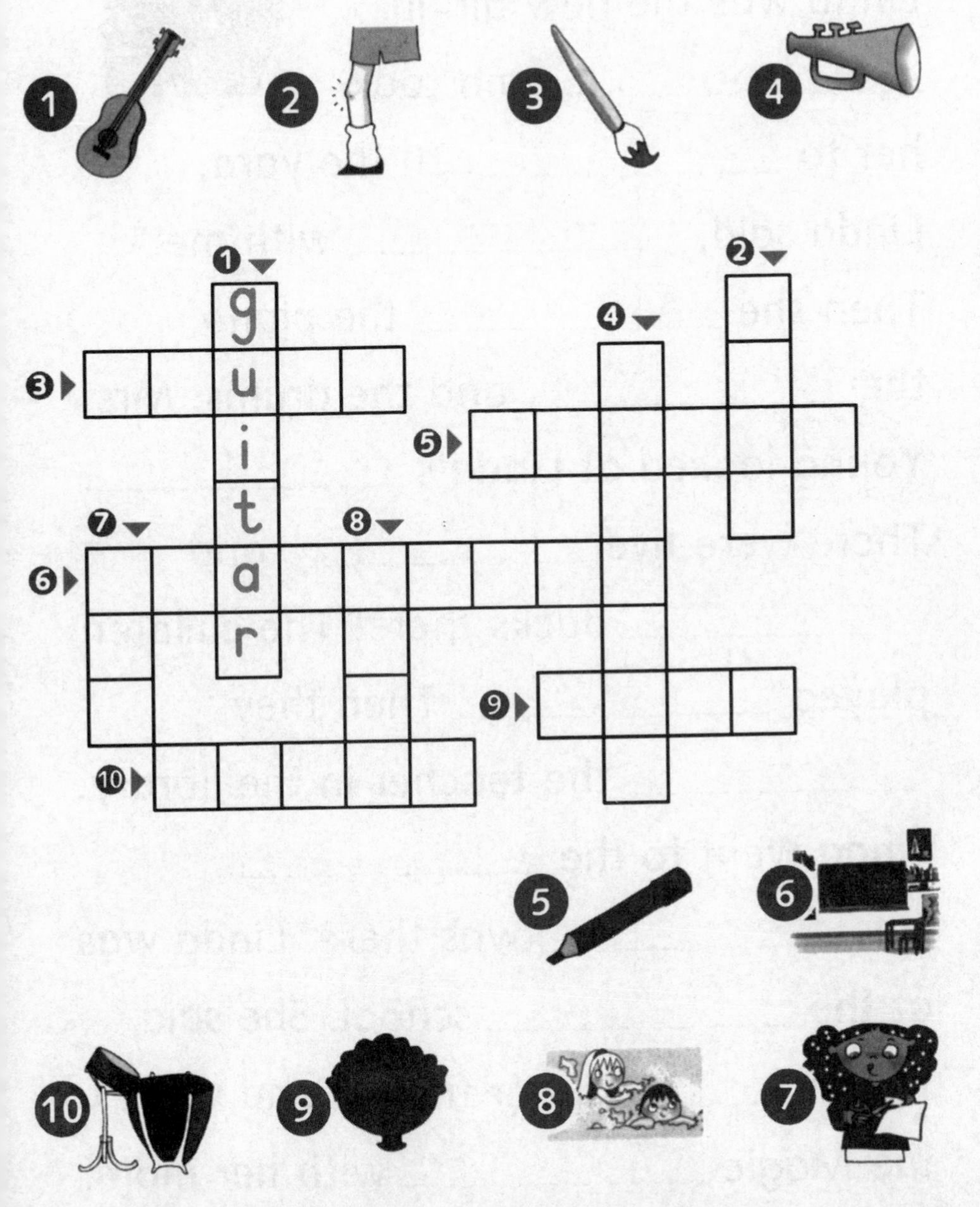

After reading

Complete the story.

Linda was the new girl in school. Emma took her to ________. In the yard, Linda said, "________ with me." Then she ________ the piano, the ________, and the drums. Mrs. Young looked at Linda's ________. There were five ________ and ________ ducks there! The children played ________. Then they ________ the teacher in the library. Linda went to the ________. Her ________ was there. Linda was at the ________ school. She said ________ to her friends and went to the Magic ________ with her mom.